PRAISE FOR

Sonnets from My Soul

"This work draws on Michelle's joy and pain through both highs and lows and countless hours, weeks, even years of soul searching, with an ardent desire to be better and to make a distinct difference in the lives of others. I hope and trust that each reader will be as blessed as I have been by the moving words and sonnets contained within."

—RONDA WILLIAMS, CEO, Brand Speaks

"*Sonnets from My Soul* is an inspiring collection of poems in which Taylor-Jones lets her imagination run free, leaving the reader with no choice but to take an introspective look at what matters most in life. Each poem offers insight that will awaken the reader's soul and propel them toward greatness."

—JACKIE GLENN, chief diversity officer,
EMC Corporation

"Taylor-Jones has an incredible gift for poetry that even she has yet to fully realize. These sonnets are beautiful nourishment to sustain the spirit within each of us."

—VALERIE IRICK RAINFORD,
author of *Until the Brighter Tomorrow: One Woman's Courageous Climb from the Projects to the Podium*;
co-founder & board chair, Black Women of Influence

"I have known Michelle since she was an ambitious college coed with a fine sense of self. I was impressed with her then and have been throughout the years. And now we have this—a moving, heartfelt surprise!"

—MATTHEW PHELAN
director of LaCerte Writing and
Academic Resource Center, Emerson College

"Michelle's voice through her poetry reminds me of Maya Angelou's quote: "You can't be what you can't see." The author sees the heart of the matter, regardless of the circumstances. Even more, these lovingly expressed reflections of life's wisdom allow us to see our truth in being human."

—TERI CAVANAGH, former executive director,
Global Banking Alliance for Women

Sonnets from My Soul

AT PEACE

A Poetry Collection

by

Michelle Taylor-Jones

Elloree Press

NEW YORK

Copyright © 2016 by Michelle Taylor-Jones

All rights reserved. No part of this publication may be reproduced, distributed, or transmitted in any form or by any means, including photocopying, recording, digital scanning, or other electronic or mechanical methods, without the prior written permission of the publisher, except in the case of brief quotations embodied in critical reviews and certain other noncommercial uses permitted by copyright law.

Published 2016
Elloree Press, New York

ISBN: 978-0-9905193-9-3

Editing & Book Design by Stacey Aaronson

Printed in the United States of America

This book is a gift to my children,

Alyssa & Tyler

and

dedicated to my parents,

Aston & Gwendolyn

for showing me that hard work, tenacity, and perseverance are values that define the character of a true champion.

I'm a woman
Phenomenally.
Phenomenal woman,
That's me.

—Maya Angelou,
from "Phenomenal Woman"

CONTENTS

Foreword i
Introduction 1

𝒞 O U R A G E

ℱear That I Know 5
𝒥ust When You Thought 7
ℰxhale 9
𝒯here Was *a* Time 11
ℱleeing Persecution 13
ℋot Tea & Scones 15
ℛunning Out *of* Time 17
𝒟on't Stop 79
ℐ Am *a* Trader 21

ℒ O V E

ℒove Has Its Limits 25
ℳy Mother's Kisses 27

Baby Girl 29
Dear Son 31
Love Trilogy 33
Your Honest Truth 35
Real Man 37

Purpose

Life 41
Garden *of* Life 43
Life Vest 45
Walking *in* Symphony I 47
Walking *in* Symphony II 49
Walk *in the* Light 51
Peace 53
Are You Ready? 55
My Mirror *of* Self-Love 57
Personal Mission Statement 59
You Are *a* Conqueror! 61

Faith

My Source 65
God's Grace 67
Stand Still 69
On My Stage 71
Preparation *for* Grandeur 73
Dash 75
Another Saturday Night 77
Fear vs. Faith 79
Joy 81

Foreword

Over the more than twenty years I've known Michelle Taylor-Jones, she would often say to me in conversations, "Vera, I'm going to write. I want to tell my story." My response to her was always, "What are you waiting for? Go for it! Someone is waiting and needs to hear exactly what you have to say."

Michelle and I talked and prayed endlessly about that dream being realized, knowing these gifts from God are meant to be shared with the world. And now, she has finally put her fears and anxieties behind her; after two decades of waiting, she has called her gifts to life.

These sonnets will remind you that even when you think God is silent, He is there for you, merely waiting for you to tap into his rest. They will elevate and inspire you to realize that there are no limits to your dreams. Whatever your heart desires, you can reach out to a higher being and He will direct your path.

In the words of Maya Angelou: "And Still I Rise." I believe Michelle's poems will give you the strength to rise too.

Vera Moore
President & CEO, Vera Moore Cosmetics

Introduction

As a small child, I was always fascinated with language. Precocious and inquisitive, I was often labeled as spoiled, and dreaming was always my escape.

I frequently wrote down my imaginative thoughts until the day my mother found my diary under my mattress and learned of my plot to eliminate her from the planet, due to her strict rules and regulations.

Though I was more cautious after that, when I discovered the ability to attach words to my dreams and create a world of my own with no restrictions, well let's just say, thus began my love affair with poetry.

It is in the most extreme moments that I do my best work. In the depths of darkness, I write of pain and despair. In the greatest of love moments, I share feelings of joy and happiness. Above all, I strive to capture a space in time that allows me to express my innermost thoughts in a way that is thought-provoking, inspirational, seductive, and even laugh-out-loud funny at times.

Despite writing for years, it is only recently that I discovered the incredible power of my words and experiences to take me beyond the moment—to reflect on both the test and the testimony.

Sonnets *from* My Soul

Writing, as it does for many people, has served as therapy for me—the exploring of experiences both good and not so good; the reflection on the language that served as inspiration for poetic justice; and the action that took me out of the darkness and into the light again to finally be at peace.

I share this collection of work in the hope that each reader will connect to at least one of my experiences and use it as a vessel in their own progression of self-discovery. Ultimately, it is my dream that you will use my poetry as a distinct and interactive approach to discovering and healing your own inner voice.

Along this path, know that although traveling through darkness may feel cold and fearful, even lonely and final, it is merely a transformation in which a rebirth is taking place. If you look deep enough, you'll find a lesson to be learned and a skill to be sharpened in preparation for a new seat at the table. That seat has been ordered for you, and a divine hand is at work ... stand still and know it was chosen by God.

Fear That I Know

The place of fear that I know
keeps me from realizing my divine order
and purpose in the world.

The place of fear that I know
paralyzes me and keeps me from walking toward the
light of my destination and abundant joy.

The place of fear that I know
doesn't contain fulfillment, resilience, or courage,
nor does it hold positive energy
or know what true happiness is.

The place of fear that I know
is dark and filled with negative voices
that create doubt and insecurities,
causing me to question my ability to be great.

The place of fear that I know
is where you will find the opposition,
the friends you no longer treasure,
apprehension and doubt that keeps you
from moving toward positivity and strength.

Sonnets *from* My Soul

The place of fear that I know
need not become a place you visit,
even for a short while,
you need not escape to this
holding space when you face doubt
or entertain those who don't lift you up.

The place of fear that I know
no longer has a resting space in my life.
I have learned to bypass this stop and instead
take a nonstop ride to abundance and glory,
for I am destined for greatness
and ready to receive it!

Just When You Thought

Just when you thought
your words could hurt me,
you learned that I use the pain to motivate my mind,
body, and spirit to be strong.

Just when you thought
your piercing eyes and divisive ways
could intimidate me,
you learned that the scripture I use as my daily guide
reminds me that
"no weapons formed against me shall prosper."

Just when you thought
your powers could limit me,
my God reminds me in prayer
that my life's purpose was created by divine design
and that his power is omnipotent.

Just when you thought
your persecution could nail me to the cross,
I ROSE UP!

Exhale

When I think about all that I hold within myself
and hide away to not make others feel less,
or insecure to be around me,
I inhale deeply.

When I think about the obstacles,
differences of opinion, pressure to do more ... or less,
or the changes I have bargained with myself to accept,
I inhale deeply.

When I think about the inner peace
I have agreed to give up,
the blessings I have decided not to utilize,
the enabling behaviors around me I have
chosen to accept for the sake of a peaceful existence,
I inhale deeply.

When I ask myself,
Am I ready to be fully present in the world?
Brilliance, beauty, and blessings abound.

Sonnets *from* My Soul

When I ask myself,
Is the world ready for what I have been designed
and divinely created to offer?

Like the rising of a magnificent sun
over the beginning of a new dawn,
I finally exhale deeply and yell out to the world ...

Yes, it is!

There Was a Time

There was a time when all I did was call out your name
and you would come to me with haste.
You were my one and only.

There was a time I didn't have to speak a word.
You felt my pain,
understood my emotions,
finished my every sentence before I spoke them.
You were my one and only.

There was a time when you fulfilled my every fantasy,
created my every dream,
completed all my thoughts,
ignited my imagination.
You were my one and only.

Now the glass is half empty,
and I yearn for it to be half full.

My trust for you has turned to darkness,
fear,
and a sense of insecurity.

Sonnets *from* My Soul

My anxiety has turned to pain
as I await the final hours of this journey.
I no longer call for you.

You no longer complete me.

We are no more.

You will never break my heart again.

Fleeing Persecution

I think about my origin, my birthright,
and my order in the universe all the time.

It allows me to pull on strength and endurance
already realized by my ancestry.

I was born of a grandmother and mother
who traveled to freedom through
the rough waters of the Caribbean Sea,
fleeing Castro's Cuba at a time of
severe upheaval and despair.

They traveled four devastating days and nights
on a small boat to freedom more than most
could endure in an hour.

Many died during the voyage,
but by rationing little food and barely enough water,
Anita Garcia and her two small children,
ages two and five years old,
made it to the safe shores of Jamaica.

SONNETS *from* MY SOUL

I lend you this memory so that
you may find your inner strength.

I hold this story deep in my soul
and pull upon it for strength,
resilience,
and the continuous will to persevere
against all odds.

Hot Tea & Scones

Propped up on the pillows in the Ritz Carlton Hotel,
the History Channel is on …

The story is an account of how blacks had to endure
slavery and horrific acts against mankind.

All of a sudden, room service knocks.

A tailored white man walks through the door
bringing me hot tea and scones
on a lovely silver platter.
Then I hear:
"Blacks were treated as though
they were less than animals."

From a distance, I hear:
"May I pour your tea, madame. Jam for your scones?"
After he leaves, I kneel down by my bedside and weep.
I say softly,
"Oh, God, look what you have done …

Sonnets *from* My Soul

Thank you Sojourner, Harriet, Mary,
Madame CJ Walker,
Michelle Obama and all my strong, magnificent sisters
who came before me,
who endured pain and suffering
so that I may enjoy hot scones on a sunny day
and the freedom and respect of a new beginning.

Running Out of Time

Today is your birthday.

Yesterday, you stopped breathing.

God allowed the doctors to revive you so that we could have more time to celebrate another year of your life.

I am not ready to let you go,
though I know I will soon have to.

I need more time,
more time to make you proud.

My children, your grandchildren,
will be graduating soon.
You have to be there.

Did I do a good enough job?

Did I do all that you wanted me to?

Did I make you proud?

I don't want you to go!

I feel like I am running out of time ...

Don't Stop

Admiring the sunrise of a new day
and being thankful for this life I have.

Laughing so hard until my stomach hurts
and tears run from my eyes.

Crying from a beautiful love story
that touches my heart.

Sharing my last dollar with a stranger
who needs it more than I do.

Caring about the world and things
that are not pretty or popular to others.

The smooth writing of my favorite pen
and capturing a beautiful memory.

Rolling down a grassy hill with my children
and hearing the echo of their laughter.

Sonnets *from* My Soul

Walking hand and hand with my love,
shoeless on a soft, sandy beach.

Eating my favorite meal until I fall back and wait
for it to digest in my enlarged stomach,
having loved every bite.

Loving my parents until all I have are beautiful
childhood memories of safety and comfort.

Being the person I was created to share with the world.

No apologies necessary ...

I Am a Trader

I am trading disgust and distance for love …
I won't allow your negative thoughts of me
to visit my mind ever again
because it blocks me from my greatness.

I am trading disappointment and resentment
that I feel toward you
for prayer over your life,
that you heal from what's missing for you
and that you find your way back onto your life's course.

I am trading sadness for empathy
because I truly understand that you cannot give
what you have never received
and that hurt people hurt other people.

I am trading blame for ownership,
owning that I allowed you into my life,
allowed you to destroy my vision of myself,
allowed you to keep me from realizing my greatness,
and that's just not okay.

Sonnets *from* My Soul

I am also trading the past for the future ...
I give myself permission to release
your negative memories from my mind,
to grab my babies and close your chapter in my life.
In forgiving you,
I am giving myself the permission to live
a brand new decade.

Call me what you want, but yes, I am a trader!

Love Has Its Limits

Why do I allow you to degrade me,
when I know you should upgrade me?

Why do I allow you to minimize,
criticize, and scrutinize me
when I know you should supersize me?

Why do I take your verbal abuse,
conversations so obtuse.
I'm so confused ...
When all other men crowd around me
for I am who they choose ...

It is the unhealthy space in which I sit,
though ashamed I must admit ...
I'm so tired of all your twisted shit.

Today I start packing up the years of nonsense,
because it's time to break away.

Now all you will have are the memories
of this beautiful love that has forever gone away.

My Mother's Kisses

My Mother's Kisses
always made me feel brave on the first day of school.
Even as an adult starting a new job,
I always went to her for my kisses
so I was sure to be okay.

My Mother's Kisses
always made all my scratches go away and feel better
even though they were not fully healed.
Even when I had a life crisis fully grown,
her kisses always made me feel that I could overcome
anything and that I was strong enough.

My Mother's Kisses
always made me feel safe when I was afraid of the dark.
I couldn't fall asleep until I knew she was near
and her kisses were close.
There are times when I close my eyes and feel
the silk of her skin against my face
and I know that she is near me.

Sonnets *from* My Soul

My Mother's Kisses
made me a giver, a nurturer, a person of compassion,
someone who listens and worries about what I can do
to help and if it will be enough.

My Mother's Kisses
made me feel secure and warm inside
and they always confirmed
the power of a mother's love.

Baby Girl

I remember when I found out I was pregnant with you;
you were due on my twenty-ninth birthday.
I couldn't believe that God was listening
to my birthday wish.

The excitement that filled my spirit at the thought
of holding you and looking into your eyes
brings me a sense of peace and joy to this day.
You are the anchor that reminds me I can love deeply
and unselfishly
and provide for a life outside myself.

For twenty-one years I have loved you, protected you,
and guided your self-awareness.
I have provided assurance that the path for your life has
been divinely created
and blessed by grace through faith.

I blinked and you went from being swaddled in my arms
to living in a world in which you are fully grown.

Sonnets *from* My Soul

My heart is filled with praise and joy
that I have poured my life into you.
Now you can share yourself with the world
and begin to soar.

I am so excited for your future as I know
your possibilities are endless.
I see your potential for greatness.

Baby girl, you are my coach, my conscience, my reality,
my strength, my positive energy, my hope,
and my best friend.

I love you more and more each day,
and I pray for our relationship
that God keeps us close to Him,
guiding our journey through life
today and always.

Dear Son

How did my ten-pound baby boy
become such an amazing young man?
I always knew one day we would get to this space in time
and you would be all grown up.

I remember the day we left the hospital
we were driving home and I thought in panic,
I can't raise a boy. We are a family of girls.
I have no idea what to do.
But together we learned and grew.

As I reflect back on the many times you gave me a fit,
I smile now because I understand that's what leaders do,
they take risks and stand up for what they believe in.

I cherish every memory,
especially when you took off in the grocery store
and I watched all the apples roll down the aisle.
Or when we had to shut down Toys R Us
in Times Square at Christmas
because you hid under the stuffed animals for an hour
playing hide-and-go-seek.

Sonnets *from* My Soul

As I recount each episode,
my heart still races at the thought of not finding you.

Fast forward and you are fully grown,
ready to show the world how magnificent
you were created to be
and how excited you are to be a force of change
in the world.

I am so proud of you, son;
you are the man I always wanted you to become.
Your future is bright, your success is palpable,
and I am your number one cheerleader.

Go forth into the world and be GREAT!

Love Trilogy

LOVE'S BEGINNING

When you hold me, I feel love's new beginning.
When you hold me,
I get lost in a space that was created for us.
When you hold me,
I surrender until our bodies meld.
When you hold me,
I become one with you.
I breathe your air, you take my breath away
and the world revolves only around us.

LOVE *on the* OTHER SIDE

In another place and time,
you look into my eyes and show me your love,
and I believe you when you say you are mine
and mine alone.

In another place and time,
you hold me, kiss me, and show me all you feel,

and I am never afraid to show you
that all my love for you is real.

In another place and time,
our laughter echoes our joy,
our love withstands all pain,
and our dreams are realized.
If only we loved in another place and time ...

LOVING YOU UNTIL THERE IS
NO MORE *to* LOVE

I will love you until my heart reaches capacity for our
love vibe and then beg you for more.

I will love you until my eyes grow tired and weary of
daydreaming about our forever plan.

I will love you until my arms grow weak from wanting
to feel your embrace and soft touch.

I will love you until we are no more ...
and I will awake from this love daydream
and start loving you all over again.

Your Honest Truth

Your honest truth would cut like a knife,
it would shut me down and often leave me vexed.

Your honest truth would send me to bed
in a spiral of midnight texts.

Your honest truth, though raw,
would put me on the right path,
simply because your honest truth was
energy intended precisely for me.

Your honest truth, though at times so painful,
taught me, freed me, loved me, and saved me.

Your honest truth is why my love for you
moves beyond eternity.

I am forever grateful for all that you gave me.

Real Man

I used to think that age determined the wisdom
of a "real man"
but you have defied all odds.

You see, somehow I truly believe you were born
knowing what manhood means,
what all the "real components" of
fulfilling life's purpose are,
to nurture and provide for the people in your life
you care about.

You are emotionally and intellectually
above and beyond most.

This sets you apart from the rest
and provides for me a space where I can come to you
and find the energy I need to survive.

You stretch me, you demand that I be my best,
you catch me when I fall but allow me
to make each mistake with open arms,
with hope that the process will teach me.

Sonnets *from* My Soul

The truth of the matter is,
I know you are a "real man"
because only when I am with you
do I feel like a "real woman."

Purpose

Life

Divorce, sick and aging parents, a health scare,
that terrible car accident …

Recounting these and other major events
that have occurred in my life,
I reflect on what it truly means to live each day out loud.

I ask myself
Were these wakeup calls for all the times
I took so many things for granted?
For the times I complained about making
homemade pizza with my children?
Now they are away at college
and I often eat pizza alone.

Or the stress of packing for family vacations instead of
cherishing the memories that would last forever.

For all the times I complained instead of being grateful.

For always planning
but never being present in the moment.

Sonnets from My Soul

Life happens whether you enjoy it or not.

There's no turning the clock back for another try at getting it right ...

So live each day out loud without regrets.

Life is way too short.

Lesson finally learned!

Garden of Life

Creating your best garden of life requires much discipline and work …
pruning, turning over soil, seeding, and nurturing with consistent light and positive energy.

Pruning:

Eliminate dead relationships
that no longer fit into your life course.
People who criticize, judge, and block you
from your blessings should be cut off.
Let that dead love go!
Free yourself from what
you already know in your heart to be true:
that you deserve better.

Turning Over Soil:

Start anew.
Build positivity into your life by making healthy choices—
mentally, physically and financially.
Focus on what pleases you and not how you please others.
Learn to say No.

Sonnets from My Soul

Seeding:

Replant and rebuild.
Add people into your life who lift you up,
people you enjoy being around because their positive
energy rebuilds your hope for a brighter future.
Hold dear family and friends who love you
in spite of your circumstances,
and those who truly want you to succeed
even if it means you soar past them.

Nurture:

Spend time caring and protecting your garden daily.
Make every effort to be good to yourself.
Add lots of light and positive energy.
Let go of the mistakes you made in the past.
Get focused, be motivated,
and start living a purpose-driven life.
Only share your goodness with people
who truly appreciate you.
The most beautiful life garden is centered
on your growth and ability to weather any storm.
Continue to blossom as you are:
"a rose by no other name."

Life Vest

Secure your life vest before you leave the house each day.

Remember to breathe ...

There will be time tomorrow
to finish what you started today.

Take off the superwoman cape,
the trophies aren't coming in the mail—
they were sent to Siberia!

We were all created to live a purposeful life.
Do so with your decisions, good intentions,
and friendships.
Set realistic goals.

Reset expectations.
Stop being a people pleaser.
That gets old real fast.

In order to fulfill the life
you were divinely created to receive,
you need to trust that you are smart, capable,

and resilient ...
that you are wrapped in a package
that is off the chain!

Make yourself a priority.
Schedule time for *you*.

Walking in Symphony 1

Are you walking in symphony with your life's purpose
in the divine steps that will lead you
to living your best life?

Are you walking in symphony with whom you are
destined to become
and not what others have proposed that you become
based on their judgment of you?

Are you walking in symphony with what you know in
your gut is what you should be doing,
or are you listening to those negative voices inside your
head that lead you to a safe place, a place of no judgment,
a place that doesn't take risks or scare you straight?

Silence the negative noise in your head
that pauses you from greatness.
Seek to understand and then be understood.
Be still and listen quietly to the signals
that life gives you when it's time to make a turn.

Sonnets from My Soul

Turn off the noise of negativisms
that block you from your blessings.
Surround yourself with only the people
who can love you despite your nonsense.
Seek goodness in your life
while giving goodness back to the world.
Then and only then will you truly walk in symphony …

Walking in Symphony II

Be in agreement with the universe.
Treat others as you would and should treat yourself:
with respect and dignity,
regardless of your title, stature, or wealth.

Be in agreement with your values.
Be not distracted by shiny objects, people, or pleasures
that bring instant fame or gratification.
Stay in agreement with what you hold
to be in line with your moral compass.

Be in agreement with a higher power,
whomever or whatever you claim
as a higher energy source.
Stand still and know that though weary your soul,
though tired your mind and body,
your journey on earth is designed for good and not evil,
to make you strong and not weak,
to provide abundance and not deplete
what you were designed to obtain.

Sonnets *from* My Soul

Eliminate and eradicate people and things from your
life that take you off course.
Life is designed to give you obstacles to climb
and negative energy to block you.
Staying on course and channeling all that is good will
provide you with clarity, connection, and commitment
to strive for a life that was divinely created
for you and only you.

Remember nothing and no one can stop your blessing
when you walk in symphony.

Walk in the Light

Realize that our spirit for living and purpose for
thriving in this universe is so much bigger
than the here and now.

Learning to own our power and our blessings
I have found to be half the battle.

The parameters that we allow ourselves and others
to use to cage us,
the restrictions we perceive to hold us down,
will never be bigger than the purpose-driven life
that has been intended for us to live out and fulfill
within our journey ...

My center and my core tells me that hope keeps us
anchored in solution and not in despair,
that all possibilities are attainable if we look beyond
all that is here and now ...

As none of us is perfect, I offer to you:

Sonnets *from* My Soul

Move forward and walk in the light
of endless promise and possibilities,
for the here and now only defines you
for a moment in time.

Your destiny has already been predetermined,
the arms you may need are there to catch you if you fall.

Let go of all that cages you
so you can spread your wings and fly.

Peace is the feeling you have at the end of a day
when you know you have done your best
and have reached out to help someone.

Peace is that walk on a warm, sandy beach,
with no one but your thoughts
as you listen to the soft serenade of the calming ocean
dancing back and forth.

Peace is being surrounded by people
who love you unconditionally
through the good times and bad,
no matter how many mistakes you make.

Peace is finding that everlasting love you long for,
that person who completes you,
as the universe confirms that this is, in fact,
your soulmate.

Peace is when you reach life's end
and you can't think of a single regret.

Sonnets *from* My Soul

You had an amazing love at least once in your lifetime,
you laughed often and until your sides ached.
You had friends you could depend on
no matter how many turns life made.
And when you take your last breath on earth,
you will embrace an eternal life
because your days on earth were fulfilled
and you are whole.

Are You Ready?

Are you ready to receive your greatness
when it shows up?
Or are you too busy with distractions,
negative thoughts,
defeatist people,
and a half-empty cup?

Greatness shows up with a quick and sneaky thrust;
it won't call your name,
or give you too many signs,
but your preparation is a must.

Be always ready, willing, and prepared
for that day you are called.
God gives us our divine course,
have nothing in your way,
for you can never be stalled.

Be not worried about walking that path alone,
slip on your heels, beloved,
and ease down that yellow brick road.

My Mirror of Self-Love

The other day I looked into the mirror
and called out my name,
but no answer echoed.

My new name screams strength,
confidence, and reassurance.

Yesterday I looked into the mirror,
but I no longer recognized myself.

I now reflect a manifestation of fortitude,
endurance,
and victory at last achieved.

Today I look into the mirror
and the person looking back at me says,
Hey you, welcome back again,
I have been here all along,
waiting for you to reclaim
the woman you were designed to be.

Personal Mission Statement

To live life understanding my full value
and purpose on earth

To love until my heart hurts from stretching,
rest, and loving hard all over again

To laugh until tears fall from my eyes
and my side aches from bending over backwards

To stare in the mirror and realize I am the most
important person to myself
and that I am a manifestation of all
that I give to the world,
and that is joy ...

You Are a Conqueror!

It is only when your blessing is near
that the evil shows up to steal, conquer, and destroy.

The purpose of evil is to block goodness and light
through jealousy, hatred, insecurity, and negativity.

The plan of evil is to weaken you through doubt,
despair, and denial
of all that is planned for your goodness.

Remain focused,
stay prayed up,
stand in conviction of your truth to endure
all that you have been created to receive ...

You are a conqueror!

My Source

Have you ever felt the dawn of a new day
as you awaken to a bright sunrise
and felt a sense of calm come over you ...
do you wonder what that is?

What about the anticipation of an amazing love
that gives you butterflies and takes your breath away
at the expectation of your next encounter ...
do you ask what could that be?

Have you ever been on the cusp of a life-altering decision
that could fall either way
but no matter which way you go,
you are excited ...
What is that invisible force?

It's energy ...

It is the source of adrenalin you feel
when you are focused, resilient, steadfast, and prayerful.
It is the invisible source that moves you to action ...

Sonnets *from* My Soul

When you are at your breaking point,
in the midst of the valley
and at the darkest point in your life,
remember to push through because that's when
God shows up to do his greatest work.

He's waiting for the opportunity to appear …
to put you on a course that was designed
for your victorious finish.
All tests are designed to reward you with a divine course,
created to multiply your life
so that you can live in abundance.

But remember …
you have to stay the course to realize
the power of your source.

God's Grace

There but for the Grace of God ...
I would have allowed this political system
that I have survived in, not thrived in, to consume me
and make me feel unworthy of all my greatness.

There but for the Grace of God ...
I would have allowed this man's insecurities,
and his need to have his ego stroked,
to make me play small in the world,
so that he would feel big in his mind ...
and other places.

There but for the Grace of God ...
I would not have been able to get up
because I believed it when he said
I couldn't survive without him,
that I would be nothing if not for him.

But only by the Grace of God ...

Sonnets *from* My Soul

did I realize with a quickness in my stride,
that my days and steps are already ordained
to endure greatness
and that God's abundant favor is upon me,
and that only goodness and mercy will I endure ...
for my mind, body, and soul belongs only in one house.

AMEN!

Stand Still

Just writing in my journal and thought of you ...

You always ask me to "be still."
It's an exercise we talk about at least once a week.

And so as I started to reflect on "being still"
and what that really means
I found myself in Psalms 46,
which says to stand still and enjoy the confidence in him
who is there in your life to provide peace.

I thought it was ironic how this verse from the Bible
spoke to me on multiple levels
and how you always represent a calm stillness
and peace in my life.

Your presence is the calming force
that God represents to the universe
as reassurance that there is a being omnipotent and
greater than the flesh of man
that directs our many paths to salvation ...

Sonnets *from* My Soul

I will stand still and know
that your arms will always be there to comfort me.
In the midst of a storm and in the depth of a valley,
I will stand still and know that it is God who leads me,
but it is you who represents the vessel he has chosen
to guide me through his word …

On My Stage

On my stage,
I will dance in the presence of fear,
for you said thy rod and thy staff will comfort me.

On my stage,
I will laugh at the persecutions and ill will,
for you said no weapons formed against me
shall prosper.

On my stage,
I will persevere and triumph in victory,
for you have anointed my head with oil
and my cup runneth over
because of your goodness and mercy.

On my stage,
You remind me that my steps are ordered,
and that they were designed
by your divine intervention.

Sonnets from My Soul

On my stage,
My star shines like a beacon of light,
and only goodness and mercy shall follow me
all the days of my life ...

as I will ALWAYS dwell in your house.

Preparation for Grandeur

Have you ever just sat still with yourself
and reflected on life?
Wondered how you got to where you are?
The journey, the people who supported you
along the way?
The advice, the mistakes, all that created the path
of learning and discovery you now claim as your life?

Life has a way sometimes of testing our resilience,
our faith, our reason for simply being
and playing well in the universe.

Becoming great in the expression
of all that we are ordained to be is an awesome task.

Some call it a test of faith, others call it luck,
while many just exist and wait for their lives to unfold.

I like to call it preparation for grandeur.

As I watch God's mighty hand at work,
I know that deliverance is amidst
and whatever comes, I shall endure.

 Dash

So I didn't get everything I wanted ...

The promotion I felt I deserved
after working hard and playing office politics.
Keeping the big house with the beautiful lawn
after the divorce.
Taking ten years instead of ten months
to lose the baby weight.

It doesn't matter!

I ask myself every day, how well did I live in the dash?

The dash between the day you are born
and the day you die.

Did you help anyone?
Did you make someone laugh?
Did you ever stop to talk to strangers and carry their
burdens while waiting on the sideline for a train?
Did you love someone? And did it feel like that deep
down in the arch of your back kind of love?

Sonnets *from* My Soul

When will you think about the short dash
of your precious time on earth
and begin to live your best life?

No one knows the length of their dash ...

Be present in the world,
for tomorrow is promised to no one.

Another Saturday Night

Another Saturday night I lie quiet in my bed
wondering how I got to this space,
questioning where and when I took that turn
I keep searching but still no trace.

I spin the corner of my mind but can't recollect
the minute, the hour, or the day.
I can't stay lost in this maze,
I must find my way.

Most days I have the weight of the world at my feet
and just can't take a step,
can't eat, can't sleep, can't think ...
lord, this load I must schlep.

Finding a way out of no way
and making it pretty is what I do,
because after all, for me it's easy,
I hold the Master's hand and he carries me through.

Fear vs. Faith

Faith: the belief of things hoped for but unseen.

Fear: the disbelief of things hoped for but unseen.

Faith and fear are in contradiction.
They cannot coexist peacefully
because they are out of balance
and cannot create a solid union.

Fear:

- people who reject you and make you never trust again
- unexpected life changes that cause you to never take a chance in life
- a love that wasn't meant to be that makes you bitter and want to never love again

Faith:

- knowing that people who reject you don't deserve your goodness in their life

- understanding that unexpected life changes are clearing your path for abundance to take you beyond what the human eye can see
- recognizing that the love you lost was in preparation for your soulmate, for someone created to grow with you and to forge a union that is unbreakable

Faith or Fear? Only you can choose your path ...

Joy

As scripture says: Weeping may endure for a night,
but joy cometh in the morning.

I bared my soul and poured my deepest self into this work
in hopes that you would find your footing
and forge ahead knowing that God's abundant grace
carried me throughout each line and verse.

I hope you will set forth with the affirmation
that no mountain is too high to climb,
and no valley too deep,
that we cannot pray ourselves out of ...

that no difficulty or strife will deter you
from marching steadfast to the end to claim victory ...

that no sickness or ill will can shake you from knowing
that our God is more than a conqueror.

Let us proclaim that life is not a destination
but a journey of progress
and that through introspective focus
and active determination toward self-improvement,
your best is yet to come!

Acknowledgments

For those of you I have blessed with my sonnets as both gift and guidance over the years, I thank you. I have shared them in good times and bad, where we often met at an intersection of my life when I needed you and you responded willingly.

The beauty of life's journey is that it teaches you who your true friends are. I have fewer people in my life on my friendship list than I have in prior years, but for those of you who have remained, I am grateful. For the few who have experienced this publishing journey with me, I send a special thank you.

To my BWOI Sisters, Marsha Haygood, Valerie Rainford, Cecilia Hurt, and Sheryl Douglas, I can't thank you enough for always supporting and encouraging me at every step. And to my friends and biggest cheerleaders, Yolanda Cook, Maritza Leites, Vera Moore, Ronda Williams, Jackie Glenn, and Ventrice Shillingford —thank you for your constant prayers and your belief in me even when I didn't believe in myself.

I also want to thank my amazing children, Alyssa and Tyler, who are my lifeline and have inspired me to be the best I can be, as well as supported me when my best wasn't quite good enough.

Special thanks to the family members who encouraged me to share myself with the world and to keep running every mile until I crossed the finish line. You are all very special, especially my niece Kimberly and my sister Jennifer.

Jenny cared for me when Mom and Dad migrated from Jamaica to the United States in search of the American Dream. She loved and sheltered me so that I would feel the security of a mother's love as best as a thirteen-year-old could do. She held me each night at bedtime until mommy came back and read me stories. She was my mother, my playmate, my friend, and above all, was and continues to be my devoted and beloved sister. It is with great appreciation for her dedicated sacrifice to care for and love me unconditionally that I truly owe her a debt of gratitude—and, in fact, my life.

About the Author

MICHELLE TAYLOR-JONES often wrote for comfort as a child, then tucked it far underneath her mattress so that no one would dare learn of her innermost thoughts. As an adult, she found her voice and has successfully built strategic plans in the areas of human resource management, community relations, sales, marketing, and diversity & inclusion.

A co-founder of Black Women of Influence (BWOI), a New York-based organization for mid-level and executive multicultural women, Michelle currently works as a human resources professional and diversity & inclusion lead. She has received numerous honors, including recognition by *Network Journal* magazine as one of "25 Influential Women in Business," and she is a sought-after speaker who has been featured in *Black Enterprise* magazine and *UPTOWN* Magazine, as well as in the media as a subject matter expert on women-owned small business banking and venture capital.

Sonnets from My Soul is her first book.

$\mathcal{I}$ WOULD LOVE TO HEAR FROM YOU!

Which was your favorite Sonnet?

Reach out to me and share at:
SonnetsFromMySoul@gmail.com

Follow me at:
www.SonnetsFromMySoul.com
@MJTSoulSonnets

Reflections

Reflections

www.ingramcontent.com/pod-product-compliance
Lightning Source LLC
Chambersburg PA
CBHW020620300426
44113CB00007B/722